NORTHERN IRELAND:
human rights and the peace dividend

National Council for Civil Liberties

acknowledgements

This report was written by Conor Foley. Liberty wishes to thank the following people for their help: Harry Cox, Martin Collins, Andrew Puddephatt, John Wadham, Jenny Watson and Jane Winter.

The report was edited by Kate Wilkinson, and designed and printed by Simon Collins.

Cover photograph: Press Association.

© 1995 National Council for Civil Liberties
All rights reserved. No representation, copy or transmission may be made without written permission.

Published by the National Council for Civil Liberties
21 Tabard Street
London SE1 4LA

A CIP catalogue record for this publication is available from the British Library.
ISBN 0 946088 53 5

contents

	page
Introduction	5
An opportunity for settlement	7
How emergency rule has eroded civil rights	10
The security forces	11
Allegations of shoot-to-kill and collusion	12
Strip searching	15
The use of plastic bullets	15
The Prevention of Terrorism Act	18
Arrests and detentions	19
Police powers	20
Examinations	21
Conditions of custody	22
Banning and prohibition	23
Exclusion orders	24
The Emergency Provisions Act	27
The Diplock Courts	28
The abolition of the right of silence	31
The Criminal Justice and Public Order Act	35
The Secret Services and accountability	37
Constitutional issues	42
Conclusion	45
Declaration on human rights, the Northern Ireland conflict, and the peace process	45
Notes	48

introduction

There is now a historic opportunity to find a peaceful settlement to the conflict in Northern Ireland.

Throughout its history, Liberty has been concerned with civil liberties and human rights in Northern Ireland. In 1935, a year after the organisation was established, a Commission of Inquiry was sent to Belfast to examine the operation of the Special Powers Act, a precursor of the modern Emergency Provisions and Prevention of Terrorism Acts. Liberty helped to establish the Northern Ireland Civil Rights Association in the early 1960s, and brought the first legal challenges to the human rights violations in the Prevention of Terrorism Act. In April 1992, Liberty helped to organise a major convention examining human rights violations in Northern Ireland, and we published the findings as *Broken Covenants* in 1993. In recent years we have been particularly concerned with the way in which policies and practices, originally developed in Northern Ireland, have seeped into public life in Britain, causing gradual but insidious damage to our freedoms. Finding a settlement to the conflict is not only an opportunity for people there to find a better life — it is an opportunity for people in Britain (and in the Republic of Ireland, which has faced similar problems) to develop better human rights practices and standards.

The human rights problems within Northern Ireland predate the recent conflict. They have afflicted Northern Ireland since its creation in 1922. Discrimination against the Catholic minority in employment and social provision, the gerrymandering of votes and oppressive policing have fuelled the underlying unresolved conflict. This is why Liberty believes that any settlement must put improved human rights standards at its heart or it will not endure. Many would argue that it was the attacks upon and suppression of the civil rights movement in the 1960s which gave rise to the conditions for the recent period of violence, which has, we hope, now ended.

Such a view is inevitably controversial. Those who identify with the historic state in Northern Ireland, and see it as the guarantor of their way of life, regard criticism of its human rights violations as an attack upon its institutions and a denial of their political legitimacy.

Liberty, however, does not take any view on the appropriate constitutional arrangements for Northern Ireland and desires no particular outcome from the current talks. We simply believe that the gun and the bomb have no place in the resolution of the conflict. We condemn all violence, from wherever it originates. Both nationalists and loyalists suffer human rights abuses; there are both nationalists and loyalists who have been sent to prison by juryless courts, who have been victims of miscarriages of justice, and who are subject to exclusion orders. Human rights problems do not come dressed in orange and green — they arise from the abuse of power by the state, directed against individuals, and they find expression in the laws and practices of state institutions.

We believe it is vital to tackle these problems. The first step is to identify the full range of issues, which inevitably means reviewing the full scale of the problem. Only by doing this will it be possible to start to identify solutions. We hope that this report can be a small contribution to that task.

Andrew Puddephatt
General Secretary, Liberty
March, 1995

an opportunity for settlement

On 1 September 1994 the Irish Republican Army announced the cessation of its campaign of military violence.[1] On 13 October 1994 the Combined Loyalist Military Command, representing the Ulster Volunteer Force and the Ulster Defence Association, announced that it was also ending its campaign.[2] On 21 October the British government said that it was making a working assumption that the IRA's cessation was intended to be permanent and that this would lead to the beginning of exploratory talks with Sinn Fein before the end of the year.[3] The British government has met representatives of Sinn Fein and loyalist groups, and discussions are continuing at the time of this report's publication. Saturday 14 January 1995 was the last day of British troops' daylight street patrols in Belfast, part of a gradual demilitarisation of Northern Ireland.[4]

The government has stated that if this demilitarisation leads to a lasting peace, it believes that many new opportunities for political advances will arise. The potential dividend of peace in Northern Ireland has four main aspects:

- **financial** — money previously spent on spent on security measures could potentially now be used to combat unemployment and poverty

- **political** — it is easier to conduct the dialogue and compromises which are the business of politics when people are not killing each other

- **civil liberties** — the government could reasonably be expected to repeal emergency laws and end the use of emergency measures as it becomes clear that the conflict is over;

- **constitutional** — there is a need for new structures of government on the island of Ireland which give democratic expression to the wishes of its people and which safeguard majority and minority rights.

The political and economic peace dividends are not within the scope of this report. We focus on the connected constitutional and civil liberties aspects of the peace dividend.

In a letter to Liberty from the British prime minister's office in November 1994 the government stated:

> Once it becomes established that terrorism has genuinely ended, there will be significant consequences for the maintenance of law and order and for the administration of justice, particularly in Northern Ireland but also in Great Britain. The government has always made it clear that the exceptional provisions in the Prevention of Terrorism Act and the Northern Ireland (Emergency Provisions) Act will remain in place only for so long as they are required by the police and courts in order to combat terrorist violence. The government will, however, need first to be satisfied that the threat which terrorism has presented to the people of the United Kingdom for the past 25 years has ended for good before taking steps to lower the nation's defences against terrorist crime.[5]

But Northern Ireland has been in a state of emergency since its inception in 1922. Many of the measures in the Prevention of Terrorism Act 1989 and the Emergency Provisions Act 1991 were in fact on the statute (in other laws), long before the conflict of the past 25 years. Other emergency laws and practices, originally introduced in response to crises, have found a wider application or have been incorporated into ordinary law.

Liberty does not believe that the threat of violence justified many of the emergency laws and practices which were implemented during the period of the conflict. They made little contribution to reducing violence and may even have helped to perpetuate it, by adding to the sense of grievance of some sections of the community. It is not an acceptable response to political violence to deny individuals their civil rights, to erode due process in the administration of justice, and to provide the authorities with powers which are unchallengeable in the courts.

Liberty is concerned that whatever constitutional settlement results, it should have at its heart the protection of human rights. We believe that State violations of internationally accepted human rights standards exacerbated the Northern Ireland conflict. Between 1959 and 1990, the British government was taken to the European Court of Human Rights more frequently than any other signatory to the European Convention on Human Rights (the ECHR), and found to be in breach of its provisions on more occasions than any other signatory.[6] Many of these violations have arisen in relation to the conflict in Northern Ireland. Britain has been found guilty of using inhuman and degrading treatment[7], arbitrary arrest[8] and failure to bring suspects promptly before a judge.[9]

Liberty supports the enactment of a British Bill of Rights. We believe that people need legally enforceable rights as protection against possible government abuses.[10] Human rights violations arising from the Northern Ireland conflict highlight the need for such entrenched protection. However, there are other ways in which the centralism and unaccountability of the British State have eroded human rights or reduced the opportunities for redress of abuses of rights. The constitutional settlement on which the United Kingdom is based is archaic and in urgent need of reform.

how emergency rule has eroded civil rights

There are three basic concerns about the administration of justice in Northern Ireland:

- the powers given to the repressive state apparatus are arbitrary and excessive
- the safeguards to protect the individual are inadequate
- the apparatus is not accountable to or representative of the whole community.[11]

The presence of soldiers on the streets and the absence of juries in court rooms provide stark illustrations of the consequences of attempting to uphold the rule of law in the absence of consent about the legitimacy of the state. But there are other consequences, in the denial of many basic human rights. There are serious concerns about Northern Ireland's inquest system[12] and police complaints procedure[13]; there is dissatisfaction at the treatment of sentenced and remand prisoners, including complaints by prisoners about the way in which their sentences are reviewed.[14] These concerns are all the more serious as they are voiced in this context: the legitimacy of the state itself is contested by a substantial proportion of the population. The ceasefire provides an opportunity for a fundamental overhaul of the State apparatus, in order to protect human rights.

Northern Ireland was created by the Government of Ireland Act 1920. This partitioned the island of Ireland and created two legislatures, both of which were intended to be subordinate to the Westminster parliament.[15] The Act passed control for policing in Northern Ireland to a subordinate parliament at Stormont in Northern Ireland. A Royal Ulster Constabulary (RUC) was established. The force was armed and given wide-ranging powers under the Special Powers Act 1922.[16] It was supplemented by an auxiliary police force, popularly known as the B-Specials. Both forces were overwhelmingly Protestant in their composition.[17]

The Civil Authorities (Special Powers) Act 1922 was based on previous British coercion acts.[18] Initially designed to be temporary, it was renewed annually and later given a five year life-span. In 1933 it was made permanent. The Act provided for arrest without warrant or charge and detention for 48 hours, indefinite internment without trial, house raids without warrant, flogging and execution, deportation, the destruction or requisition of property, the blocking of roads, curfews, the prohibition of inquests and the banning of organisations, meetings and publications.[19] The Home Secretary was also empowered to introduce additional regulations, by decree, if the government considered them necessary for the preservation of law and order.[20]

The security forces

In 1969 British troops were re-deployed on the streets of Northern Ireland, for the first time since the 1920s. In August 1971 internment without trial was re-introduced, having previously been used intermittently by the police. In 1972 Northern Ireland's Stormont parliament was discontinued during a general outcry after soldiers of the Parachute Regiment shot dead 14 civil rights protesters in Derry.[21] From 1972, Northern Ireland has been governed directly from Westminster.

Government policy since the mid-1970s has been to place primary responsibility for security in the hands of the police and to expand the roles of the Royal Ulster Constabulary (RUC) and the Ulster Defence Regiment (UDR). However, the British army still has a highly visible presence in west Belfast, Derry city, parts of Tyrone and south Armagh. Their presence remains a source of frequent tensions and conflict.[22] Since the ceasefire this presence has been scaled down but it is still noticeable. The behaviour of soldiers has led to many other complaints, particularly against soldiers of the Parachute Regiment.[23]

Problems also exist in relation to the police force. In March 1969 the government's Cameron Commission conducted an inquiry into policing in Northern Ireland.[24] Its report led to the establishment of the Hunt Committee which made a series of recommendations for reforms: the disbanding of the B-Specials and the creation of a new part-time reserve force, the disarming of the RUC, the establishment of a Police Authority and the repeal of much of the Special Powers Act.[25]

The attempt to create a civilianised police force lasted until November 1971, when the RUC was rearmed. The B-Specials were abolished in April 1970 and replaced with the Ulster Defence Regiment (UDR). This was integrated into the regular army and it was hoped that it would live down the sectarian reputation of its predecessor. However, the proportion of Catholics in the UDR declined rapidly, from around 20 per cent in 1970 to less than three per cent by the 1980s.[26] In 1992 the UDR was merged into the Royal Irish Rangers (RIR). But even after the merger, the new regiment's composition is still less than six per cent Catholic.[27]

Allegations of shoot-to-kill and collusion

A recurring problem during the conflict was the allegation that special units within both the police and army operated an unofficial shoot-to-kill policy. Over 330 people were killed by the security forces during the conflict.[28] A survey by international lawyers in 1985 concluded that in 155 of the 269 deaths it investigated, the people killed had no paramilitary connections.[29] In some other cases it has been alleged that the security forces killed people when they could have arrested them or killed people after first wounding them.[30] Article 6 of the International Covenant on Civil and Political Rights (ICCPR) states that no one should be arbitrarily deprived of the right to life. Article 2 of the ECHR specifies that a deprivation of life is only justifiable when it is "absolutely necessary" in strictly defined circumstances.[31] However, in Northern Ireland the security forces may use lethal force "as is reasonable in the circumstances".[32]

Only four soldiers have been convicted of murder while on duty in Northern Ireland. One of them, Ian Thain[33], who killed a civilian in 1985, spent two years and three months in prison before he was released and allowed to rejoin his regiment. The conviction of the other soldier, Lee Clegg, who killed a teenage woman joy rider in 1990 has been the subject of a vigorous lobbying campaign.[34] In February 1995 two soldiers were sentenced to life imprisonment for the murder of a Belfast teenager in 1992.[35] In the same month a soldier, Andrew Clarke, fired 20 bullets into a crowd of mourners outside a dead IRA member's house. He hit one person twice, who was wounded but not killed. Clarke received a 10-year prison sentence.[36]

International attention was focused on the alleged shoot-to-kill policy by the SAS killing three unarmed IRA members in Gibraltar in 1988[37], and six fatal shootings carried out by an RUC special unit in Armagh in 1982. These six deaths resulted in the establishment of an inquiry headed by a Manchester police officer, John Stalker. He encountered obstruction and deceit involving senior RUC and MI5 officers before his dramatic removal from the investigation on disciplinary charges, which were later proved to be fabricated.[38] The report was concluded by another police officer but its findings have never been made public and the inquests into the deaths have had to be abandoned.[39]

There have also been numerous complaints about the behaviour of the UDR, both on patrol and in relation to alleged collusion between some of its members and loyalist paramilitaries.[40] Nationalist politicians have demanded that the regiment be disbanded.[41] In 1989 the Deputy Chief Constable of Cambridgeshire, John Stevens, conducted an inquiry following claims made by the Ulster Defence Association (UDA) and Ulster Volunteer Force (UVF), in the same year, that they were receiving high quality information from military, police and intelligence sources enabling them to murder suspected republicans.[42] The inquiry concluded that information had been passed by members of the security forces to loyalist paramilitaries, and had been used in planning or carrying out attacks. It also concluded that the passing of such information was neither widespread nor institutionalised, although leakages of information may never be completely eliminated.[43]

These conclusions have been rejected by some observers. One study looked into 99 killings by loyalist paramilitaries between March 1990 and 1992. It concluded that 88 had either a political or sectarian motive and in 48 cases there was some evidence of collusion with the security forces.[44] At least two loyalist paramilitaries, Albert Baker and Brian Nelson, have claimed that they worked under the direction of military intelligence. In Nelson's case the British army has admitted that he was one of its agents, but denies that it used him to set up targets for assassination. He did, however, hold a senior position within the UDA, was involved in arranging a massive shipment of arms to loyalists from South Africa and would have had prior knowledge of many of the UDA's murder plans.[45]

The extent to which the authorities may have tolerated or promoted collusion remains debatable. One of the most controversial incidents was the murder of a defence solicitor in Belfast in 1989 after a highly publicised accusation by a government minister that members of the legal profession were colluding with terrorists. In January 1989 a parliamentary committee debated the amendments to the Prevention of Terrorism Bill, in which the government was seeking to overturn the normal confidentiality between solicitors and their clients. A government minister, Douglas Hogg, declared that:

> I have to state as a fact, but with great regret, that there are in Northern Ireland a number of solicitors who are unduly sympathetic to the cause of the IRA. [interruption] I repeat that there are in the Province a number of solicitors who are unduly sympathetic to the cause of the IRA. One has to bear that in mind.[46]

He was immediately challenged by a nationalist MP, Seamus Mallon, who said that Douglas Hogg's remarks threatened the entire legal profession in Northern Ireland, and that "it will be on the head of the Minister and government if the assassin's bullet decides to do, by deed, what this government has done by word."[47] Hogg refused to retract or substantiate his remarks but repeated the allegation several times, in virtually identical language, claiming that he had received guidance from "people who are dealing in these matters."[48] Less than a month later a well-known Catholic solicitor, Patrick Finucane, who specialised in criminal defence work, was murdered by loyalist paramilitaries.[49]

Finucane had represented both loyalist and republican suspects but had come to public attention during a number of high profile cases involving republicans. He represented a man who was injured during one of the shootings John Stalker investigated. Stalker was criticised by an RUC sergeant for attempting to talk to Finucane during his investigation. The sergeant told Stalker "[Finucane] is an IRA man — any man who represents IRA men is worse than an IRA man. His brother is an IRA man also and I have to say that I believe a senior policeman of your rank should not be seen speaking to the likes of either of them."[50] One of Finucane's brothers had received a prison sentence for IRA activities, but there is no evidence that Finucane was himself involved in the IRA. However, the RUC clearly disliked him intensely. There were a number of reports of the RUC naming him and other solicitors as IRA men to people whom they were interrogating.[51]

Strip searching

Systematic strip searching of Irish women prisoners was introduced in the early 1980s against women remand prisoners in Armagh gaol.[52] Nothing of any security value was found on these women, who were stripped naked twice a day. Many complained that the anguish they suffered on their way to and from court appearances affected their ability to prepare for their trials.[53] In 1983 the authorities announced that they were abandoning routine strip searching, but would still carry out random strip searching.[54]

As recently as March 1992 (in fact on International Women's Day), the authorities carried out a mass forcible strip search of women prisoners in Maghaberry Gaol. The search, conducted by officers in riot gear, lasted 10 hours. Twenty-one prisoners who resisted were forcibly stripped. Up to six prison officers held down individual women. Nothing of security value was found.[55]

There have been continued protests that strip searching constitutes inhuman and degrading treatment and violates the right of people held in detention to be treated with respect for the inherent dignity of the person. Women prisoners who have been granted compassionate leave to attend the funeral of a family member have been strip searched on their way into and out of prison.[56] Women detained under the Prevention of Terrorism Act, most of whom never face charges, are also often strip searched.[57]

The use of plastic bullets

Seventeen people have been killed by plastic and rubber bullets in Northern Ireland.[58] Hundreds have sustained serious injuries. Eight of those killed have been children.[59] The use of plastic bullets has been condemned by politicians from both communities in Northern Ireland. A resolution calling for them to be banned was overwhelmingly carried by the European Parliament in 1982.[60]

A plastic bullet is as heavy as a cricket ball but harder. It leaves the gun at 160 miles per hour. It is designed for crowd dispersal and the security forces maintain that most of those who have been killed were rioters.[61]

The three people to be killed by rubber bullets were Francis Rowntree, aged 11, in April 1972 in Belfast; Tobias Molloy, aged 18, in July 1972 in Strabane; and Thomas Friel, aged 21, in May 1973 in Derry. Fourteen people have been killed by plastic bullets:[62]

name	age	date	place
Stephen Geddis	10	August 1975	Belfast
Brian Stewart	13	October 1976	Belfast
Michael Donnelly	21	August 1980	Belfast
Paul Whitters	15	April 1981	Derry
Julie Livingstone	14	May 1981	Belfast
Carol Ann Kelly	12	May 1981	Belfast
Henry Duffy	45	May 1981	Derry
Nora McCabe	30	July 1981	Belfast
Peter Doherty	33	July 1981	Belfast
Peter McGuiness	41	August 1981	Belfast
Stephen McConomy	11	April 1982	Derry
John Downes	22	August 1984	Belfast
Keith White	20	April 1986	Portadown
Seamus Duffy	15	August 1989	Belfast

The high number of deaths in 1981 coincided with widespread street protests during a hunger strike by republican prisoners. John Downes was killed when the RUC tried to force its way through an anti-internment anniversary rally in 1984. Keith White (the only Protestant on this list), was shot during loyalist protests against the Anglo-Irish Accord in 1986. In 11 out of these 14 cases the police's claim that the victim was rioting has been contested by witnesses or by the judge or coroner at the inquest into their deaths.[63]

Only one RUC officer has been prosecuted for causing a death. He was acquitted even though it emerged at his trial that the bullet was fired in contravention of the rules.⁶⁴ In 1988 Standard Fireworks, then the principal supplier of plastic bullets to the Ministry of Defence, announced that it would cease production, after a meeting with relatives of people killed and injured by the bullets.⁶⁵

There have been no fatalities from plastic bullets since 1989, but they have caused many horrific injuries. The security forces have continued to use plastic bullets since the ceasefire. For example, in October 1994 in Belfast, one man had to be placed on a life support machine after his skull was fractured by a plastic bullet fired from a distance of about 10 yards.⁶⁶ The bullet was fired after a confrontation between a group of youths and a joint RUC and army patrol, during which, the security forces claim, they came under attack. In the same month a man was hit on the leg by a plastic bullet in Cookstown during a mini riot outside a hotel. It was claimed that the RUC fired into the crowd indiscriminately.⁶⁷ The continued use of plastic bullets since the ceasefire is particularly worrying and sets a dangerous precedent for policing public order situations. Liberty believes that the use of plastic bullets should be banned.

the prevention of terrorism act

The Prevention of Terrorism (Temporary Provisions) Act (the PTA) was introduced to parliament on 25 November 1974, four days after bombs in Birmingham pubs killed 21 people. The Home Secretary at the time acknowledged the Act's powers were so draconian as to be "unprecedented in peacetime". During the debate, it was estimated that the Act would be in force for about six months.[68] The Act was passed in 42 hours, virtually without amendment or dissent. Over 20 years later, the Act is still on the statute book, having been re-enacted in 1979, 1984 and 1989. Some of its provisions have been modified, but its basic powers remain largely unchanged.

According to the government's statistics, the Act does little to combat terrorism. More than 7,000 people have been detained in Britain under the Act, but the vast majority have been released without charge. Three per cent have been charged with offences under its provisions, between five and six per cent have been charged with other offences and four per cent have been excluded or deported.[69] Almost without exception the people who were charged with terrorist-related offences could have been arrested under ordinary criminal law.[70]

In his memoirs, Sir Robert Mark, who was Chief of the Metropolitan Police when the PTA was enacted, stressed that at the time the police regarded the Act as primarily a political measure:

> It was introduced by the Home Secretary because he felt a need to reassure the public of the willingness of the government to take firm measures in the face of Irish terrorism. The police were largely indifferent. The NCCL were quite right in assuming that we would not let any legal niceties prevent us from dealing with terrorism and that we were therefore not all that interested in what we thought was essentially a propaganda measure. In fact the real beneficiaries were the one and a half million decent Irish people living and working in this country who were overnight relieved of the embarrassing spectacle of their intellectually subnormal compatriots collecting money for

the IRA or indulging in childish melodramatics on their behalf. That was about the only real benefit afforded by the Act, but I have no doubt the Irish minority were grateful for it. . . The new Act was undoubtedly helpful in that it curbed the activities of the civil libertarians who are always so anxious to bomb, to maim and to kill.[71]

Arrests and detentions

From 1990 to 1993 inclusive, the numbers of people arrested and charged under the PTA in Britain were as follows:[72]

year	arrested	charged				excluded/ deported	not charged	not charged as % of arrests
		offences under PTA	'terrorist' offences[73]	theft	other			
1990	193	6	–	–	22	16	163	84
1991	153	4	–	–	3	11	144	94
1992	160	9	7	4	18	3	124	77
1993	152	5	17	1	9	4	120	79

These figures give rise to serious concern. The majority of charges brought under the PTA are for offences such as refusing to co-operate with an examination, breaching an exclusion order or withholding information. None of these offences is serious.

Of the people who face charges brought under other Acts, only a minority faces charges that can be reasonably considered to be terrorist-related — murder, possession of firearms or explosives, conspiracy to commit murder, explosions or arson. Most face charges for other offences, such as possession of cannabis, possession of stolen goods, and social security fraud offences. While these are crimes, they hardly justify the retention of the PTA's draconian provisions.

Police powers

Under Section 14(1) of the PTA the police may arrest without a warrant any person "who is or has been concerned in the commission, preparation or instigation of acts of terrorism." This involvement can be "active" or "passive".

Section 14(1) is a major departure from ordinary criminal law. Generally a warrantless arrest may only take place if the police have reasonable suspicion that a specific arrestable offence has been committed and that the individual they are arresting committed this offence. Because no crime has to be specified under Section 14(1), the police have been given greatly increased powers of arrest. Individuals being questioned or facing criminal charges, and their lawyers, may not know the specific crime of which they are suspected.

Arrests usually take place either at ports of entry into the country or following police raids. Often these are carried out in high-profile and dramatic fashion. People have had their front door smashed in during the early hours of the morning and have been dragged from their bed at gun-point.[74] Such raids employ excessive and unreasonable force, they stigmatise the person being arrested and ensure that people are frightened and disorientated when they arrive at the police station. These objections are compounded by the fact that ordinary criminal law is quite sufficient to deal with situations where the police have reasonable suspicion that the person they are arresting is armed and dangerous.

Liberty is concerned that arrests can be made without evidence that the arrested individual has committed a specific crime. The experience of the raid is likely to be traumatic for the person, and damaging to their reputation with friends, neighbours and colleagues. Such arrests can lead to the loss of jobs and homes and it is not uncommon for individuals to suffer abuse or assaults after detention. Some detainees have experienced long-term psychological traumas after their release and there are cases of suicides being linked to detentions.[75] If charges are brought, the person's chances of receiving a fair trial may be prejudiced by such a high-profile arrest. And we emphasise again that the overwhelming majority of people arrested under the PTA are innocent of terrorist involvement.

Liberty has documented many cases in which people have been arrested in these circumstances, often after terrorist attacks, only to be released without charge, explanation or apology.[76] In summer 1993 Liberty made British legal history when it extracted an apology from the Metropolitan police and compensation for wrongfully arresting a group of young people.[77]

Under Section 18 of the PTA it is a criminal offence to withhold from the police information about terrorism and terrorists. This offence erodes the right of silence, since the police can threaten to charge people with it if they refuse to answer all of the police's questions. Charges under this section have been infrequent and it has been suggested that it has been used mainly against people whom the police suspect — with little evidence — to be involved in terrorist activity.[78] However, there have been complaints that it has been used to intimidate relatives of people whom the police suspect of involvement in terrorist activity.[79] In a review of the operation of the PTA Lord Shackleton commented:

> There are genuine doubts about its implications in principle and about the way it might be used in the course of interviewing someone. . . it has an unpleasant ring about it in terms of civil liberties.[80]

Section 18 of the PTA has also been used to force the media to hand over footage and information relating to terrorist activities.[81] There have been few prosecutions, but in 1992 Box Productions and Channel Four Television were fined £75,000, for refusing to comply with an order to identify a source for allegations in a programme about collusion between members of the security forces and loyalist paramilitaries.[82]

Examinations

Schedule 5 of the PTA confers powers of detention at ports of entry in Britain and Northern Ireland on police, immigration officers and custom officials. An individual may be questioned for up to 12 hours if the officer has no suspicion about the individual, and up to 24 hours if the officer has reasonable suspicion as defined under Section 14. After the first hour of the examination the detaining officer must record that the individual is being detained, inform him or her in writing of their right to contact a lawyer, and notify a relative.

In determining whom to examine, the police and port authorities routinely screen millions of travelling people every year. In a review of the PTA, Lord Colville estimated that approximately one million people were stopped at ports of entry each year and questioned briefly by an officer, or made to fill out an embarkation card detailing their name and address, occupation, nationality, purpose of travelling and details of where they will be staying.[83]

An alarming feature of the Act is that it allows the police and other officers to hold people at ports for up to an hour without having to record this fact. During this time people can be subjected to intrusive and intimidatory questioning, and miss a connecting train, boat or plane, without this fact being recorded anywhere.

Conditions of custody

The first people arrested under the Act were three young Irish men and a teenage English woman who all signed statements, after extended periods of detention, confessing to other pub bombings earlier that year.[84] The Guildford Four, as they became known, served 15 years before their convictions were quashed.

People detained under Section 14 of the PTA can be held in 24-hour solitary confinement for up to seven days without access to a court. The Home Secretary, or the Secretary of State for Northern Ireland in the case of detentions in Northern Ireland, must authorise the extension of a detention beyond the first 48 hours. Detentions of seven days are in breach of Article 5 of the European Convention on Human Rights and the British government has been forced to derogate from this Article (that is, set it aside, because the UK cannot ensure the protections it specifies).[85] This derogation was supported by the European Court of Human Rights in May 1993, on the grounds that an emergency existed in Northern Ireland which was sufficiently serious to justify the denial of these rights.[86] It is doubtful whether the European Court would accept that grounds for derogation still exist, now that the ceasefire has come into effect. Extended detentions clearly breach the spirit of international law.

In England and Wales the custodial regime for a person detained under the PTA is expressly tied to the Code of Practice for the Detention, Treatment and Questioning of Persons by the Police, which is contained in the Police and Criminal Evidence Act 1984.[87] Similar rules operate in Scotland via police force orders. There is also a Code of Practice made under the Emergency Provisions Act 1991 (the EPA), which governs the treatment of detainees in custody in Northern Ireland.

Because the PTA allows extended detentions, issues of diet, bedding and exercise take on an added importance. A detained individual is unlikely to see natural light or have the opportunity for proper exercise for up to seven days. There have been many complaints from individuals who allege that their sleep was interrupted, that they lost track of whether it was day or night, that their cells were too hot or cold, that their food was inedible, that they were denied washing facilities and that they were denied reading or writing material.[88]

Following the release of the Guildford Four in 1989, more and more police forces in Britain are recording interviews on tape.[89] However, the government refuses to make it a requirement to video and tape-record all interrogations of individuals detained under the PTA in Britain and Northern Ireland, in spite of persistent complaints from detainees of threats, physical abuse and fabrication of evidence.[90]

Detained individuals can be denied access to a solicitor for the first 48 hours of their detention and may be questioned in the absence of one. A 1993 study by the Home Office into PTA detentions in Britain found that access to legal advice was delayed in over a quarter of all cases in which detainees asked for it, and that in a substantial minority of cases no grounds were given for this delay.[91] Only 19 per cent of all foreign nationals were informed of their right to communicate with their embassy.[92]

In Northern Ireland it is particularly difficult for solicitors to gain access to their clients. The police can also refuse to notify a detainee's friend or relative for 48 hours. The PTA enables the police to use "reasonable force" to photograph and fingerprint detainees without a court order and without their consent. Files on detainees can be kept even if they are released without charge.[93]

Banning and prohibition

Under Section 1(2)(a) of the PTA, the Secretary of State may proscribe any organisation which "appears to him to be concerned in, or in promoting or encouraging terrorism occurring in the United Kingdom and connected with the affairs of Northern Ireland." The power to proscribe is entirely at the discretion of the Secretary of State. No evidence need be produced and no appeal is permissible. The Secretary of State does not need to refer the matter to parliament before proscribing an organisation. The organisations currently proscribed under the PTA are the Irish Republican Army and the Irish National Liberation Army.[94] Membership of a proscribed organisation is an offence under Section 2 of the Act, punishable by up to 10 years imprisonment.[95] Supporting a proscribed organisation is also an offence.[96] Section 3 specifies that this includes displaying items of support for a proscribed organisation, such as badges or T-shirts, soliciting or receiving money, for example by holding a collection box, arranging or addressing a meeting of more than three people in support of the aims of a proscribed organisation, and inviting non-financial support for the organisation.

Proscription makes very little difference to the activities of paramilitary organisations, which by their nature operate in a clandestine fashion. And as the list of activities illustrates, the powers of proscription are far more likely to be used against political supporters of republicanism or loyalism than against those involved in paramilitary activity. Implementation of Section 3 has not been consistent. People have been arrested for selling republican newspapers, badges or calendars that have been tolerated in other cases. The powers are in any case rarely used. Between 1974 and 1990 there were only three charges brought under Section 3, two of which were withdrawn, and seven prosecutions under Section 2, which resulted in two convictions.[97] There were no prosecutions under either section between 1990 and 1994.

The argument against proscription is that terrorist actions should be (and are) criminalised, and not involvement in political organisations. Government advisors have accepted that prescription makes very little contribution to combating terrorism, and have rejected adding other organisations to the list of groups proscribed under the PTA.[98]

Exclusion orders

Section 5(1) of the PTA empowers the Home Secretary to make an exclusion order if it appears to him or her that an individual "is or has been involved in the commission, preparation or instigation of acts of terrorism to which this Part of the Act applies." The terms "preparation" or "instigation" are vague, and can include planning, encouragement, or direct involvement. The terms of the Act allow an exclusion to be made if the individual may have been involved in terrorism in the past or could have an intention to be involved in terrorism in the future.

British citizens cannot be excluded from the United Kingdom entirely but can be restricted to living in Britain or Northern Ireland. This section effectively creates a system of internal exile. Irish citizens who do not have British citizenship can be excluded from the whole of the UK. It is a criminal offence, punishable by up to six months imprisonment, to break an exclusion order.[99]

Exclusion orders are made entirely at the discretion of the Home Secretary, who acts on the advice of the police. The order includes no explanation of why it is being served. Exclusion orders are based on secret evidence, often in the form of uncorroborated statements, the accuracy of which it is impossible to judge. A person subject to an exclusion order has no right to know the evidence on which it was made, no right to examine that evidence, to offer a defence or to have the case heard in public. A person subject to an order may appeal by requesting an oral hearing before an adviser appointed by government, under Schedule 2 paragraph 3(1). The excluded individual has no right to legal representation. The Home Secretary has a duty to take into account the report of this adviser, but has no obligation to inform the individual of the reasons for the success or failure of the appeal.

The majority of people who have been excluded from Britain still live and move freely in Northern Ireland, which has led to complaints that the area has been turned into a "dumping ground." Unionist politicians have said that it is repugnant that the government believes some people too dangerous to allow into Britain, yet places no restrictions on their movement in Northern Ireland.[100]

People who have been subject to exclusion orders are stigmatised as terrorists without ever appearing in court on formal charges and ever having the opportunity to clear their names. For example, in October 1993 John Matthews was re-arrested and served with an exclusion order, after terrorist-related charges against him had been withdrawn.[101] Liberty has also received complaints from individuals who have attempted to leave Northern Ireland to get away from the problems of political violence, only to be served with exclusion orders which oblige them to remain there.[102]

The UK can not ratify Protocol 4 of the European Convention on Human Rights, which provides for freedom of movement and settlement within one's own country, because of exclusion orders. The UK is the only country in Europe to have a system of imposing internal exile on its own citizens.[103] The UK has also had to enter a reservation on the application of Article 12 of the ICCPR (which sets out the right to freedom of movement), to the effect that the right of freedom of movement shall apply separately to each of the territories of the UK.[104] This means that people have the right to move within England, Scotland, Wales and Northern Ireland but not necessarily between these territories.

On 4 March 1993 a person subject to an exclusion order was granted leave for a judicial review in the Court of Appeal, challenging exclusion orders as a breach of Article 6 of the ECHR (the right to a fair trial), and of European law on the free movement of labour.[105] In July 1994 Liberty won a referral to the European Court of Justice in Luxembourg, of a case brought on behalf of Sinn Fein's president, Gerry Adams. The grounds for referral were that exclusion orders may violate the right of freedom of movement contained in European Union law.[106]

Since the ceasefire, exclusion orders served on Gerry Adams and Martin McGuinness, another leading Irish republican, have been lifted. Exclusion orders against John Gallagher and Kevin McQuillan, both the subject of legal challenges,[107] have also been lifted. However, the power of exclusion remains and continues to offend against international human rights standards.

On 29 November 1994 the government announced that 61 exclusion orders remain in force and stated that:

> the government hope that the day is approaching when exclusion orders will no longer be needed but we are not prepared to lower our guard prematurely.[108]

Liberty believes that the continued use of exclusion orders is no longer justified.

the emergency provisions act

The Northern Ireland (Emergency Provisions) Act 1973 (known as the EPA) was enacted following the report of a commission chaired by Lord Diplock. It was established to consider "what arrangements could be made in order to deal more effectively with terrorist organisations... otherwise than by internment."[109] Most of the Commission's recommendations were enacted in the EPA, in spite of criticism that its examination had been cursory and overly dependent on the British army's assessment of the situation.[110]

The EPA's provisions only apply in Northern Ireland. The EPA was amended in 1975 and re-enacted in 1978 and 1987. Before 1987 most emergency arrests in Northern Ireland took place under the EPA, but since then the security forces have relied upon the powers contained in the PTA.[111] Internment was gradually phased out in 1975 as the authorities made more use of the new powers in the PTA and EPA, although the power to order internment remains in the EPA. In 1961 the European Court of Human Rights clearly stated that it is a breach of the ECHR to hold someone in detention to prevent them committing criminal offences without bringing the accused before a court, and without the intention to hold a trial.[112] A further challenge to internment was upheld by the European Court in 1978.[113]

A new EPA was passed in 1991 which repealed the previous legislation but re-enacted most of its provisions and incorporated the powers of the PTA that only applied to Northern Ireland. It also created two new offences: going equipped for terrorism and possession of information likely to be of use to terrorists. These are discussed further in this report, in the section on the Criminal Justice and Public Order Act 1994.

The 1991 EPA re-enacted other provisions contained in the Special Powers Act giving the security forces extended powers to stop, search, question, arrest and detain people and to block roads.[114] The EPA gives soldiers the power (unique in UK law) to arrest and detain people for up to four hours.[115] The EPA also gives the Secretary of State for

Northern Ireland the power to ban organisations,[116] though there are few prosecutions for membership or support of proscribed organisations.[117]

The Diplock Courts

The EPA creates a separate legal regime for people arrested on suspicion of committing what are known as "scheduled offences" — principally crimes of violence, attacks on property, explosives and firearms offences, theft, intimidation, blackmail and membership of a proscribed organisation.[118] There are special provisions governing notification of arrest and access to solicitors. If people are charged with these offences they are tried in what are known as "Diplock Courts". These have no juries, there are special rules governing the admissibility of some evidence and the burden of proof is reversed in some charges (that is, innocence is not presumed and must be proved).[119] Originally these courts were envisaged as a temporary measure to deal with the problem of intimidation of jurors and perverse jury verdicts (that is, usually, verdicts in which the jury acquits in spite of the evidence). However, this original justification was at the time vigorously challenged.[120]

Most significantly the EPA lowers the standard for the admissibility of confessions which may have been obtained through improper means. While under the Police and Criminal Evidence Act 1984 confessions must automatically be excluded if they have been obtained "by oppression of the person who made [them]"[121], under the EPA they remain admissible provided that they have not been obtained through torture or inhuman or degrading treatment or violence or the threat of violence.[122] Judges in Northern Ireland retain some discretion to exclude confessions which have been improperly obtained but it is unclear what other physical ill-treatment a suspect could have to undergo before any statement would be ruled inadmissible.

Between 1976 and 1979 the Diplock Courts achieved a 94 per cent conviction rate. The vast majority of these convictions rested wholly or mainly on confessions signed by suspects while in police custody.[123] Concern about the treatment of detainees grew after it was revealed that a selected group of the first internees in 1971 had been subjected to special interrogation techniques. These included being made to stand spread-eagled against a wall, being hooded, being subjected to continuous noise and being deprived of food and sleep for days on end. In 1976 the European Commission on Human Rights found that

Britain had tortured these "hooded men". A ruling by the European Court of Human Rights in 1978 amended the verdict to that of using inhuman and degrading treatment.[124]

By the late 1970s a number of human rights groups were registering concern about alleged ill-treatment suffered by detainees in attempts to force them to sign confessions while they were in police custody. In 1978 Amnesty International published a damning report.[125] The British government responded by setting up its own inquiry, chaired by Lord Bennett. It reported the following year that a number of detainees suffered injuries which could not have been self-inflicted.[126]

After 1979 the number of complaints about ill-treatment fell but rose again at the end of the 1980s and the start of the 1990s. A 1991 Amnesty report stated that "existing procedures and safeguards are inadequate to prevent the ill-treatment of detainees."[127] In 1991 Amnesty International also issued an urgent action notice over ill-treatment of a 17-year-old youth in Castlereagh. The United Nations Committee on Torture has expressed its concern about the regimes operating in Northern Ireland's holding centres.[128] The Strasbourg-based Committee for the Prevention of Torture, set up by the Council of Europe, has accused the British government of permitting psychological and physical ill-treatment of detainees, including assaults and death threats, during police questioning.[129]

There are also clear difficulties in a system which has a judge, in a court with no jury, considering the admissibility of evidence and also deciding what weight should be attached to that evidence. These difficulties have been highlighted by the RUC's reliance on confession and accomplice evidence. In cases involving these types of evidence, it is usual for a judge to warn the jury about the reliability they should attach to such testimony. Defence lawyers often succeed in having them excluded from the trial. In the absence of a jury, Diplock Courts sometimes witness the bizarre spectacle of a judge stating that he is warning himself that the evidence he is about to consider may be unreliable.[130]

During the early 1980s several hundred people were charged in Northern Ireland on the basis of uncorroborated statements by alleged accomplices. A series of mass trials in the Diplock Courts occurred in what became known as the "supergrass" system.[131] The supergrasses (informers) were all former paramilitaries and in most cases had been induced to testify, by promises of a shorter sentence for their own crimes or payments of up to £100,000. Many were shown to have a history of perjury or psychotic behaviour. In 1984 and 1985 a number of supergrass trials collapsed and other convictions were overturned in the Court of Appeal. Some supergrasses admitted that they had been put under pressure to supply as many names as possible, that they had named people that they had never even met, had substituted names and had simply signed statements drawn up by the police.[132]

Judges became more sceptical of supergrass evidence and fewer became willing to give evidence. Some observers concluded that a policy decision had been taken to abandon the "system". The existence of a system was denied by the authorities, who have always insisted that the emergence of people they preferred to call "converted terrorists" had been spontaneous. However, some supergrasses who retracted their evidence claimed they had been threatened with long prison sentences on falsified charges or that the security forces would set them up to be murdered.[133] The emergence of the "supergrass system" highlighted serious concerns about the criminal justice system in Northern Ireland, pointing to the need, which still exists, for thorough reform.

the abolition of the right of silence

On 20 October 1988 the Secretary of State for Northern Ireland, Tom King, announced that he would bring forward measures to abolish the right of silence for people arrested in connection with scheduled offences in Northern Ireland.[134] He claimed that this right was regularly being abused by hardened terrorists to frustrate the police and prosecuting authorities. He alluded to a trial which was taking place at the time in Britain in which he himself was the alleged victim of a terrorist conspiracy.[135] The day before this announcement the three defendants in this trial had chosen not to give evidence. There has been speculation that the announcement's timing was deliberately designed to influence the trial's outcome.[136] All three defendants were convicted but in 1991 these convictions were quashed on the grounds that King's announcement had infringed their right to a fair trial.[137]

In November 1988 the House of Commons approved the Criminal Evidence (Northern Ireland) Order. This removed the right of suspects in Northern Ireland to remain silent under police questioning and at trial without adverse inferences being drawn.[138] Tom King referred to "the acknowledged difficulties faced by the police and prosecuting authorities in bringing to justice hardened, professional criminals — often assisted by able legal advisors."[139] The Criminal Evidence (Northern Ireland) Order was an Order in Council, a type of "delegated legislation", which can only be accepted or rejected by parliament and is not open to amendment. The use of this to abolish the right of silence was criticised at the time by the Conservative MP Ian Gow and subsequently by the Standing Advisory Committee on Human Rights, amongst others, because of its inadequate opportunity for parliamentary scrutiny and debate.[140]

The right of silence is a centuries-old safeguard against wrongful convictions and oppressive questioning.[141] The new law permits a judge, jury or magistrate to draw such inferences as they think fit from a suspect's failure to mention, at the earliest possible moment under police questioning, facts which are material to their defence, or from their failure to account for anything else which might connect them with a crime.[142]

The law also requires courts to call on defendants to give evidence at trials and gives the courts the power to draw adverse inferences from defendants' failure to do so.[143] Silence may also be treated as corroborative evidence against the accused.[144]

Abolition of the right of silence has increased the concern felt by many criminal justice practitioners and human rights activists in Northern Ireland about the risk of wrongful convictions.[145] It is of particular concern because of the legal regime governing the arrest, detention, interrogation and trial of people accused of scheduled offences in Northern Ireland. A person arrested in connection with a scheduled offence in Northern Ireland may be denied access to their legal representative for 48 hours. Solicitors cannot sit in on interviews and interviews are not tape-recorded. In one case the courts ruled that adverse inferences can be drawn from the failure of a suspect to answer questions, even if he or she has requested legal advice before making a statement.[146]

In 1994 a challenge to this ruling was declared admissible by the European Commission of Human Rights, on the grounds that it breached the ECHR.[147] The Commission decided that the denial of access to a solicitor was a breach of the ECHR. It also decided that in this instance, the fact that adverse inferences could be drawn when he failed to answer the police's questions or give evidence at his trial, did not mean that the complainant had been denied the right to a fair trial; however, this fact had to be seen in the context of the strength of the case against him as a whole. In the circumstances of this particular trial the Commission decided that the loss of the right to silence did not constitute a breach of the ECHR, but Convention case law makes clear that all the facts and circumstances of each case have to be considered in order to decide whether an applicant has had a fair trial. The UK Commissioner noted, in his opinion on the decision, that it would be more difficult in a non-jury court to ensure that there were adequate safeguards to ensure that proper inferences were drawn from a defendant's silence than it would be in courts in which a judge had to give direction to a jury.[148]

The Committee on the Administration of Justice (CAJ) has documented a number of cases in Northern Ireland in which it believes the safety of the conviction is in doubt. In these cases, either adverse inference was drawn from the silence of the defendant, or the defendants may have been induced to make false confessions because they feared that their refusal to answer all the police's questions would be held against them at their trial.[149]

Vulnerable and naive suspects are believed to be particularly at risk of miscarriages of justice because of the abolition of the right of silence. A new caution warns people of the consequences of their responses to police questioning, but there is concern that it is little understood and widely misinterpreted, and that it has placed undue pressure to speak on suspects.

A study was carried out in 1994 by CAJ and Justice, the British section of the International Commission of Jurists, to inform the debate about the proposal in the Criminal Justice and Public Order Act 1994 to abolish the right of silence in England and Wales. It confirmed these concerns and also found that the abolition of the right of silence has not reduced crime or improved charge and conviction rates.[150] The government's figures show that the proportions of people caught and convicted of recorded crimes have actually dropped since the abolition of the right of silence. "Clear-up" rates for crimes (that is, the percentage of crimes reported for which someone is charged with an offence) peaked at a record high of 45 per cent in 1988, but fell in each successive year after the abolition of the right of silence. They were 11 per cent lower in 1992 than before abolition of the right to silence.[151] Conviction rates also dropped. They were three to four per cent lower in the four years after the abolition of the right of silence than in the four years before it.[152]

The CAJ and Justice study noted that judges initially showed considerable caution about how much weight they gave to the fact that a defendant had chosen to remain silent at some point in police custody or during the trial. However, it noted a "real and pronounced" shift in the burden of proof which judges were requiring when applying the Criminal Evidence (Northern Ireland) Order, "which almost takes silence as presumptive of guilt."[153]

The study concluded that the Order "offends the principles of self-incrimination and presumption of innocence" and "raises serious considerations on whether the provisions of the Order can be compatible with the right to a fair trial enshrined in Article 6 of the European Convention of Human Rights."[154] However, it also stated that:

The government's main argument for change [in England and Wales], in 1994 as in 1988, rests on the likelihood of charging and convicting more people, particularly serious and habitual criminals. The available evidence from Northern Ireland gives no ground for supposing that has been the case there, or will be in England and Wales. On the contrary, the statistics support the opposing views advanced during the debate, and supported by all the research evidence into the actual effect of silence in the United Kingdom: that as a weapon in the fight against crime, the abolition of the right of silence is of little use.[155]

the criminal justice and public order act

On 3 November 1994 the Criminal Justice and Public Order Bill became law.[156] The Act abolishes the right of silence in England and Wales for anyone accused of any criminal offence. It increases the powers of the police in a variety of situations, reduces the rights of defendants and it creates a number of new criminal offences.

The Act confers stop and detention powers on the police in Britain which are similar to those the police and army currently possess under the Northern Ireland (Emergency Provisions) Act 1991. Under Section 81 of the Act a police officer of commander rank can authorise the stopping and searching of people in a particular location for a period of up to 28 days, "where it appears" to him or her "that it is expedient to do so in order to prevent acts of terrorism." This became law after the republicans and loyalists had both declared their ceasefires. The police can also stop any vehicle and search it, as well as its driver and passengers, and stop and search any pedestrian for "articles of a kind which could be used for a purpose connected with the commission, preparation or instigation of acts of terrorism."[157] The Act specifies that "A constable may, in the exercise of those powers, stop any vehicle or person and make any search he thinks fit whether or not he has any grounds for suspecting that the vehicle or person is carrying articles of that kind."[158] The Act makes it a criminal offence to refuse to co-operate with a stop and search.

Once an operation has been authorised, the police do not need to have any suspicion, reasonable or otherwise, that the person that they are stopping has any involvement with terrorist activity or is guilty of any specific crime. There is no objective test of a just cause for the detention. Instead, if it "appears" to a police commander "that it is expedient to do so", all police officers in a given area will be given the power to stop and search people, on the grounds that they are "preventing terrorism."

Before the enactment of the Criminal Justice and Public Order Bill, the City of London police had established road blocks around the city of London, in July 1993, and were carrying out random checks on motorists.

They claimed to be acting under powers contained within the Road Traffic Act,[159] but Liberty believes they were in fact exceeding their powers. Liberty received complaints from people who objected to being stopped, and has gathered anecdotal evidence that some people were arrested for technical motoring offences and that black people were frequently being detained.[160] In response to a complaint from a member of the public, the Acting Commander of the City of London wrote:

> I note your comments about black people being stopped. Many members of the public who are stopped may not necessarily fit the current profile of a terrorist, however, terrorist tactics are constantly changing and we must be alert to all possibilities.[161]

In November 1994 the police issued statistics for the number of vehicles stopped for which details are recorded (which is significantly less than the total number of vehicles stopped).[162] The figures show that the overall number of stops has fallen, but the proportion of black people being stopped has risen sharply. Between 1 July 1993 and 31 December 1993, 4,595 drivers had their details recorded, of whom 82 were black: 1.7 per cent of the total. Between 1 January 1994 and 31 July 1994, 3,949 drivers had their details recorded, of whom 254 were black: 6.4 per cent of the total. Between 1 August 1994 and 31 October 1994, 1,446 drivers had their details recorded, of whom 159 were black: 10.8 per cent of the total.[163] These figures illustrate how intended "anti-terrorist" measures erode civil rights, and can disproportionately affect particular groups in society.

Section 82 of the Act creates two new offences. A person is guilty of an offence if he or she is in possession of an article "in circumstances giving rise to a reasonable suspicion" that it is intended "for a purpose connected with the commission, instigation or preparation of acts of terrorism."[164] A person is also guilty of an offence if he or she is found to be collecting or possessing, without authorisation, "any information which is of such a nature that it is likely to be useful to terrorists."[165] Both of these offences carry a maximum sentence of ten years. There is no requirement that the person who has material intends to use it for terrorist purposes. This new offence is likely to be of particular concern to campaigners, journalists and other researchers, who might in certain circumstances have to prove that information they were collecting could not be of use to terrorists. This would be a formidable legal challenge.

the secret services and accountability

The Northern Ireland ceasefire provides an opportunity for reviewing the role and accountability of the UK's Secret Services. There is real concern that, with the end of the cold war and in the absence of a conflict in Northern Ireland, the Security Services will extend their remit into ordinary criminal investigations without being subject to adequate democratic scrutiny and control.[166]

During 1994, Stella Rimmington, head of the internal Security Service MI5, conducted a public lobbying campaign to gain support for extension of the organisation's role. In an annual lecture in June 1994 she set out her view of the organisation's future after the Cold War and the "dramatic" diminishing of the "threat of subversion." In the past, Rimmington said, MI5's principal task had been to counter the espionage of the Soviet Union and its allies. MI5 had also "set out to identify all the members of these subversive groups (Trotskyists and Communists) and to investigate their activities."[167] But now, she said, less than five per cent of the organisation's time is spent on monitoring political subversion. MI5's most important task, which takes up nearly half its resources, is now "mounting intelligence operations to counter the threat from Irish terrorism."[168]

The second largest area of MI5 operations, international terrorism, accounts for 26 per cent of its work and has been mostly concerned with the Middle East. She said that "the threat to British interests from terrorism of international origin is lower than it was in the 1980s" but she believed it remained a significant threat. She singled out "extremists from North Africa and also Kurdish groups" as posing an increasing threat.[169] This could signal the start of operations by the Secret Services against some ethnic minorities, particularly the Kurdish community which has been targeted for special surveillance.[170] The lack of accountability in the way MI5 operates, and their track record in combating Irish terrorism, are serious causes for concern about this potential development.

In November 1994, following the ceasefire by the IRA and loyalist paramilitaries, Rimmington said, in a speech to a police officers' conference, that MI5 would be taking an increasingly active part in criminal prosecutions.

She said that she saw no reason for any overall reduction in its activities, and that MI5's "distinctive role" was:

> the way that we use secret sources and techniques to find out what those who we are investigating are at pains to conceal. . . [T]he immediacy of the terrorist threat in recent years has focused attention on the potential for integrating secret intelligence into the judicial process. . . The question now arises about what role the Security Service should play in the prosecution of such crimes.[171]

Stella Rimmington also admitted that: "It is almost inevitable that national security intelligence work, which is based on the use of covert sources and techniques will involve some infringement of the civil liberties of those who are under investigation."[172] In 1992 MI5 was given primary responsibility for Northern Ireland counter-terrorism within Britain, which had previously been the preserve of the Special Branch.[173]

MI5 did have some notable successes between 1992 and 1994, with a greatly increased arrest rate, but some of their techniques were controversial. In the first case that came to trial in which MI5 had been involved, it was revealed that MI5 operatives had set up and largely financed a bogus terrorist operation.[174] Inert explosives had been placed in a quarry in Somerset by an MI5 operative after he had been approached by the Irish National Liberation Army (INLA), two of whose members were subsequently arrested attempting to break into the quarry in order to steal the explosives. The cars, a safe house and metal cutting equipment used in the operation were all supplied by MI5. In another trial it was alleged that MI5 operatives had allowed bombs to go off in London and the bombers to escape back to Ireland although they were constantly under surveillance during the time that they were in Britain.[175]

The trials were marked by the appearance of MI5 agents in court as anonymous witnesses and the use of Public Interest Immunity (PII) certificates (certificates that the Home Secretary signs, advising the trial judge that certain information is too sensitive to be disclosed to the defence). Liberty believes that, despite the safeguards that exist, the use of secret intelligence and anonymous witnesses during criminal trials infringes the right of defendants to a fair and public hearing. The use of PII certificates, in all trials in which MI5 are involved, is a particular concern.

In August 1994 the Court of Appeal upheld the right of defendants to see and know the identity of their accusers, including witnesses for the prosecution.[176] However, the court ruled that this right could be set aside in exceptional circumstances at the judge's discretion.[177] This could pave the way for increasing involvement by secret agents in criminal prosecutions. It could lead to an increasing number of criminal trials featuring agents giving evidence from behind screens. In December 1994 MI5 officers gave evidence at another trial involving suspected IRA members. They were completely obscured from the press and public gallery by screens, brown paper and masking tape.[178]

MI5 is barred from disclosing to anyone any of the material or intelligence that it has gathered on individuals. The Security Services Act 1989, which placed MI5 under statutory control, permitted one exception to this ban. It specified:

> that there are arrangements for securing that no information is obtained by the Service except so far as necessary for the proper discharge of its functions or disclosed by it except so far as necessary for that purpose or for the purpose of detecting serious crime.[179]

However, the Intelligence Services Act 1994 extended this and enabled disclosure "for the purpose of any criminal proceedings."[180] This signalled MI5's increased willingness to involve itself in criminal prosecutions, including allowing its operatives to appear as prosecution witnesses. In October 1994 it was reported that MI5 had taken control of all investigations into computer hacking and abuse in Whitehall.[181] This action, taken without reference to parliament, gives the Secret Service formal access to all Whitehall computers, including the Police National Computer (PNC) and personal information about millions of people.

In her November 1994 lecture Rimmington also said that the relationship between MI5 and the Special Branch was "closer than ever", and she referred to guidelines published by the Home Office in the same week on relations between the two organisations. These specified that the Special Branch had a duty to gather "accurate assessments of the public order implications of events such as demonstrations" and suggested that the force should monitor the activities of people who might cause violence at such events.[182] The Special Branch is sometimes described as "the eyes and ears of MI5."[183] The two forces perform similar functions although, unlike MI5 operatives, Special Branch officers have powers of arrest.

The Special Branch operates with minimal accountability or public scrutiny. MI5 and the Special Branch have their own liaison officers in different parts of the country and it is normal practice for these to deal directly with each other and to bypass the local chief constable.[184] A Special Branch commander has told a Home Affairs Select Committee that he "did not think it in the public interest" to reveal how many files they kept on people[185] but it is estimated that between them MI5 and the Special Branch hold about three million personal records on computer.[186] A former police Chief Constable, John Alderson, has said that about half the files held by the Special Branch in his area should not have been held.[187] Considerable concern has been expressed about people being labelled as "subversive" and continuing to have their movements monitored simply because they took part in a perfectly legitimate protest 10 years previously.[188]

In the context of the Northern Ireland conflict it is understandable why the authorities keep many operational details confidential, although the government's refused to divulge even how many Special Branch officers there are in Northern Ireland seems difficult to justify.[189] However, the use of an internal secret police force to enforce ordinary criminal law raises a number of civil liberty concerns.

The scrutiny and democratic accountability of the Secret Services in particular are totally inadequate and its agents are not subject to statutory rules of conduct and evidence. The existence of MI5 was not even officially acknowledged until 1989 when the Security Service Act placed it on a statutory footing. Stella Rimmington is the first head of the organisation to appear in public and it was not until July 1993 that the service published a booklet setting out its structure.[190]

The Security Services are not accountable to parliament or the public. There is a Commissioner who reviews their operations but parts of his reports are never made public.[191] There is a tribunal to deal with individual complaints but it has never upheld a single one and can never give reasons about its decisions or reveal anything to the complainant about their case.[192] The Intelligence Services Act 1994 created, for the first time, a parliamentary committee with limited scrutiny powers over the operation of MI5, MI6 and GCHQ. However, it cannot examine operations, it can be denied access to "sensitive" material, and it reports to the prime minister rather than to parliament. Its members are also appointed and can be dismissed by the prime minister.[193]

The Northern Ireland ceasefire provides an opportunity for scaling down this unaccountable security work. However, there is a danger that these practices will simply be extended into the criminal justice system or used against legitimate political protesters.

constitutional issues

The fundamental cause of the Northern Ireland conflict has been the conflicting views of its inhabitants about the territory's constitutional status. Liberty does not take a view on Northern Ireland's long-term constitutional status. However, we do believe that discussion about how the territory is governed should be informed by a human rights perspective and that there are important lessons to be learned from Northern Ireland's experiences about the protection of human rights.

From a negative point of view, Northern Ireland's experiences show the failure of the existing British constitutional arrangements to protect fundamental human rights and freedoms. Since its inception, Northern Ireland has failed to uphold the rights of all its population to equal treatment before the law. Emergency laws and practices have violated international human rights standards. There has been widespread social, economic, cultural and political discrimination against Northern Ireland's minority Catholic community.[194]

Between 1922 and 1972 Northern Ireland was governed by a devolved parliament at Stormont,[195] although ultimate sovereignty remained with the Crown in parliament at Westminster. Certain subjects were reserved for the UK, including treaties and foreign relations, the armed forces and defence, nationality, postal services, customs and excise and income tax.[196] It has been argued that Northern Ireland's experience of devolved government sharply illustrated the limitations of the Westminster model of government. The system was characterised by majoritarianism — that is, the mistreatment of the minority (Catholic in this case) by the (Protestant) majority — which was facilitated by a strong executive unchecked by safeguards for minority rights.[197]

Since 1972 Northern Ireland has been governed directly from Westminster. There is a Secretary of State for Northern Ireland, who sits in the British Cabinet, but, like the Welsh and Scottish Secretaries, is not accountable to the people he or she governs. The Secretary of State has direction and control of virtually all the powers of decision-making relating to Northern Ireland. Most laws made for Northern Ireland take the form of Orders in Council. These are introduced by the Secretary of State, as a type of what is known as "delegated legislation". They must be accepted or rejected in their entirety because they cannot be amended by parliament.[198] And many powers, which are the responsibility of local authorities in the rest of the United Kingdom, are vested in unelected quangos in Northern Ireland. Northern Ireland has 161 appointed executive quangos and concern has been expressed at their lack of openness and their varying degrees of accountability.[199]

In 1985 the Hillsborough Agreement granted the Irish government a consultative role in running the affairs of Northern Ireland. This has provided a mechanism for airing the grievances of the minority community as well providing institutional recognition of the constitutional aspirations of the minority community in Northern Ireland.

In December 1993 the British and Irish governments agreed a declaration which stated that:

> It is for the people of Ireland alone, by agreement between the two parts respectively, to exercise their right to self-determination on the basis of consent, freely and concurrently given, North and South, to bring about a united Ireland, if that is their wish. . . It would be wrong to attempt to impose a united Ireland, in the absence of the freely given consent of a majority of the people of Northern Ireland. . . the democratic right of self-determination by the people of Ireland as a whole must be exercised with and subject to the agreement and consent of a majority of people of Northern Ireland.[200]

Following the IRA and loyalist ceasefires the governments and political parties are seeking agreement on new proposals within the next two years which will then be put to a referendum. A framework document for discussion, published by the UK and Irish Governments as this report goes to press, proposes:

- a devolved assembly for Northern Ireland, elected by proportional representation
- a new North/South body of elected representatives of the Northern Ireland assembly and the Irish parliament
- a parliamentary forum of representatives of the Northern Ireland assembly and the Irish parliament to hold wider discussions

- amendments to the British and Irish constitutional claims over Northern Ireland to incorporate the principle that any change in its constitutional status can only come about with the consent of its people
- increased co-operation between the British and Irish governments through the inter-governmental conference established by the Hillsborough Accord
- guarantees by both governments to protect the civil, political, social and economic rights of the people of Northern Ireland.[201]

These proposals are likely to be the subject of lengthy discussions and will eventually be put to the people of Ireland in two separate referenda, both of which will require majority support.

Northern Ireland can also offer some positive lessons in rights for British society. One legacy of the civil rights movement is that there is a highly developed rights culture in Northern Ireland.[202] All the political parties in Northern Ireland support the introduction of a Bill of Rights and most believe that merely incorporating the ECHR into domestic law would not itself provide adequate protection.[203] Northern Ireland also contains bodies such as the Standing Advisory Committee on Human Rights[204] and the Fair Employment Commission which could act as potential models for a new Human Rights Commission in Britain with enhanced powers to promote human rights. Increased co-operation between the British and Irish governments and the possible creation of new institutions covering the whole of Ireland may also mean that an all Ireland human rights organisation will be needed, to scrutinise their activities.

The UK does not have any anti-discrimination legislation relating to Northern Ireland beyond the Fair Employment (Northern Ireland) Acts 1976 and 1989. The Race Relations Act 1976 does not apply in Northern Ireland. The UK has adopted the stance of the Geneva Conference on Security and Co-operation in Europe (CSCE) which guarantees the rights of minorities to express, preserve and develop their culture. However, the UK abstained in the vote to accord the draft European Charter for Regional or Minority Languages the legal form of a convention. The UK recognises minority rights in section 5(a) of the Anglo-Irish Agreement.

conclusion

The history of Britain's involvement in Ireland shows that temporary measures have become entrenched, exceptional powers have been normalised and laws and institutions originally introduced to deal with Irish insurgencies have subsequently found wider applications.

The British government's record before the European Court of Human Rights shows that many of the measures introduced in relation to Northern Ireland would probably have breached a British Bill of Rights had there been one. One lesson from the conflict is that the doctrine of parliamentary sovereignty has failed to protect human rights during crises. Any new settlement must respect the differing aspirations of the peoples on the island of Ireland and have at its heart the protection of legally enforceable rights against government abuse.

On 9 December 1994, the following organisations adopted a *Declaration on human rights, the Northern Ireland conflict, and the peace process:* the Committee on the Administration of Justice, Irish Council for Civil Liberties, Liberty, Scottish Council for Civil Liberties and British Irish Human Rights Watch. The text of this declaration follows.

Declaration on human rights, the Northern Ireland conflict, and the peace process

Firm and effective legal protection of human rights and civil liberties, and the creation of a culture in which everyone's human rights are respected, are crucial if the peace process is to succeed.

For too long human rights abuses have been regarded as normal in Northern Ireland and increasingly in the neighbouring jurisdictions as well. The failure of the legal and political systems to address such abuses has left its mark on the conflict, creating a climate of abuse, oppression and fear. At this historic moment, there is a unique opportunity to put in place new structures which will defend and promote human rights.

The effects of the conflict have not been confined to Northern Ireland but have also led to the introduction of draconian legislation and practices in the Republic of Ireland, England, Scotland and Wales. In

order to dismantle oppressive laws and practices, the following minimum changes are urgently required in all these jurisdictions:
- emergency legislation must be repealed
- special courts must be abolished
- the right to silence must be restored
- political censorship must be ended for good and the legislation which allowed it repealed
- all forms of discrimination must end and comprehensive anti-discrimination legislation must be introduced
- military personnel should play no further part in policing and all forms of covert operations must be ended
- Castlereagh and other holding centres for persons detained under emergency legislation must be closed and extended detention periods ended
- an urgent review must be conducted in partnership with local communities into all security barriers and surveillance installations
- there must be a planned review of the sentences of all those imprisoned under emergency legislation.

All those involved in negotiating a new political framework for Northern Ireland must recognise the central role of human rights and civil liberties if there is to be a just and lasting peace in the longer term. New systems of justice are required which will address the injustices of the past and ensure rights for the future.

In particular:
- A broadly-based and fully representative Commission on Policing must be instituted to examine the nature, structure and methods of policing in Northern Ireland with a view to producing a model of policing which is representative of and has the confidence of all sections of the community and which is impartial, just and fully accountable.
- A fully independent system for investigating complaints against the police must be established.
- A Bill of Rights must be enacted which protects the rights and liberties of everyone.

- The criminal justice system in Northern Ireland should be thoroughly and independently reviewed and, where necessary, changed.
- An independent Commission of Investigation must be instituted in order to investigate human rights abuses arising from the emergency legislation.
- Human rights education and awareness must become an integral part of every school curriculum and training programme.

Respect for human rights and civil liberties must be made an integral part of any political settlement and the political process must include all the communities in Northern Ireland. Everyone there is entitled to be engaged and involved in the peace process and to have his or her rights guaranteed as part of any new political settlement.

Just as the conflict in Northern Ireland has led to emergency laws and assaults on democratic rights and freedoms in all the jurisdictions in these islands, so the opportunity must now be taken not just to dismantle this apparatus of repression, but to put in place safeguards which will prevent any similar erosion of human rights and civil liberties in any of these jurisdictions in the future. To that end, we will work to ensure the adherence of the two governments to all relevant international human rights conventions and standards.

Human rights belong to everyone, being universal and inalienable. Our societies, our legal systems, and our political processes should affirm and guarantee that guiding principle.

notes

1. *An Phoblacht/Republican News,* 1 September 1994, statement issued in the name of P O'Neill, Irish Republican Publicity Bureau, Dublin.
2. *Guardian*, "Loyalists order a ceasefire", 13 October 1994.
3. *Daily Telegraph*, "Major agrees to talks with Sinn Fein", 22 October 1994.
4. *Sunday Times*, "Farewell to arms lures big money to Ulster", 15 January 1995.
5. Letter from 10 Downing Street, 4 November 1994.
6. *A People's Charter, Liberty's Bill of Rights, A Consultation Document,* National Council for Civil Liberties, 1991, at 113. Between 1959 and 1990, the European Court gave 37 judgements against the British Government and found that it had violated at least one article of the Convention on 27 occasions. The next most frequent offender, Austria, has been in breach on 15 occasions. In 1991 Italy overtook Britain as the most frequent violator and Britain now ranks second.
7. *Ireland v UK* (1978) Case No. 5310/71
8. *Fox, Campbell & Hartley v UK* (1990) Case Nos. 1224/86 and 12383/86.
9. *Brogan and others v UK* (1988) Case Nos. 11209/84, 11234/84, 11266/84.
10. For details see National Council for Civil Liberties, 1991.
11. See, for example, *Human rights in Northern Ireland,* Helsinki Watch, 1991.
12. For details see *Inquests and disputed killings in Northern Ireland,* CAJ, 1992.
13. For details see *Police accountability in Northern Ireland,* CAJ, 1988.
14. For details see *Life sentence and SOSP prisoners in Northern Ireland,* CAJ, 1989.
15. For details see Frank Pakenham, *Peace by ordeal,* Mercier Press, 1951.
16. For details see Chris Ryder, *The RUC: a force under fire,* Octopus, 1990.
17. For details see Michael Farrell, *Arming the Protestants: the formation of the Ulster Special Constabulary and the Royal Ulster Constabulary 1920-27,* Pluto Press, 1983.
18. Gerard Hogan and Clive Walker, *Political violence and the law in Ireland,* Manchester University Press, 1989, at 14.
19. Civil Authorities (Special Powers) Act 1922, Section 5, Schedule 1-5 Regulations 7a, 18a, 22a, 23a, 24a. Also Regulations 18c (1923), 26a (1930), 8a (1931), 4 (1933), 22b (1933), 24c (1933).
20. *Ibid.*, Section 1(3)
21. For details see *Report of the Tribunal appointed to inquire into the events on Sunday 30 January 1972 which led to the loss of life in connection with the procession in Londonderry on that day* (The Widgery Report) and *Justice Denied, a challenge to Lord Widgery's report on Bloody Sunday,* the Defence and Education Fund of the International League for the Rights of Man in association with the National Council for Civil Liberties, 1972. Thirteen of the protesters died on the day of the shootings and the fourteenth subsequently died after being wounded.

22. For details see Robbie McVeigh, *Harassment, the security forces and young people in Northern Ireland*, CAJ, 1994.

23. *Andersonstown News*, "Paratroop peace", 19 November 1994.

24. *Disturbances in Northern Ireland: report of the Commission appointed by the Governor of Northern Ireland* (The Cameron Report), HMSO, 1969, Cmnd 532.

25. *Report of the advisory committee on police in Northern Ireland* (The Hunt Report), HMSO, 1969.

26. For details see Chris Ryder, *The UDR*, Methuen, 1991.

27. *Hansard*, the Army Bill, 13 February 1991, cols 1185-1186. Relating to the UDR and the Royal Irish Rangers immediately before the merger.

28. *Observer*, "Irish special", 11 July 1993.

29. For details see Kader Asmal (Chairman), *Shoot to kill? International Lawyers' inquiry into the use of firearms by the security forces in Northern Ireland*, Mercier Press, 1985, at 125.

30. For details see Fr Raymond Murray, *The SAS in Ireland*, Mercier Press, 1990.

31. The UK has ratified both the ECHR and the ICCPR but has not signed the Optional Protocol of the ICCPR which would allow people the right to take individual cases to the UN. However, the government must submit a report to the United Nations Human Rights Committee every five years outlining how it is complying with the Covenant.

32. s3(1) the Criminal Law Act 1967.

33. *R v Thain* (1985) 11 NIJB 31 (CA).

34. *Guardian*, "Where justice lies bleeding for decades", January 1995.

35. *Independent*, "Guardsmen get life for Belfast murder", 11 February 1995.

36. *Andersonstown News*, "Pathetic", 11 February 1995.

37. For details see Harry Kitchin, *The Gibraltar Report*, National Council for Civil Liberties, 1989.

38. For details see *The Stalker Affair, more questions than answers*, CAJ, 1988 and John Stalker, *Stalker*, Harrap, 1988.

39. *Guardian*, "Coroner abandons 12-year 'shoot-to-kill' inquests after court refuses access to Stalker report", 9 September 1994.

40. See *Amnesty International Concerns in Europe*, "Killings by the Security Forces in Northern Ireland", May 1992-October 1992, at 87-90. Also *Human Rights Concerns in the UK*, Amnesty International, 1991, at 34-38. See also Murray, 1990.

41. See for example, *Hansard*, Army Bill, 13 February 1991, cols 1151-1215.

42. For details see *Summary of the report of the Deputy Chief Constable of Cambridgeshire John Stevens, into allegations of collusion between members of the security forces and loyalist paramilitaries*, Cambridgeshire Constabulary, 1990.

43. *Ibid*.

44. For details see *Shoot to kill and collusion*, Relatives for Justice, 1993.

45. BBC programme *Panorama*, "Dirty War", broadcast 8 June 1992.

46. *Hansard*, Standing Committee B, 17 January 1989, col 508.

47. *Ibid.*, col 519.

48. *Ibid.*

49. For details see *Legal defence in Northern Ireland, following the murder of Patrick Finucane on 12 February 1989*, Report of an international delegation of lawyers, 1989.

50. Stalker, 1988, at 49.

51. *In defence of the defence, fourth report to the United Nations special rapporteur on the independence of judges and lawyers concerning attempted intimidation of defence lawyers in Northern Ireland*, British Irish Rights Watch, 1994.

52. For details see *Strip searching, an inquiry into the strip searching of women remand prisoners at Armagh Prison between 1982 and 1985*, the National Council for Civil Liberties, 1986.

53. *Hansard*, Written Answers, 29 July 1983, col 631 and 5 December 1983, col 84.

54. National Council of Civil Liberties, 1986, at 15.

55. *Just News*, "Non-sense of security", CAJ, April 1992.

56. National Council of Civil Liberties, 1986, at 6.

57. Paddy Hillyard, *Suspect community, People's experiences of the Prevention of Terrorism Acts in Britain*, Pluto Press, 1993, at 157-159.

58. For details see *Plastic bullets and the law*, CAJ, 1990.

59. For details see *They shoot children, the use of rubber and plastic bullets in the north of Ireland*, Information on Ireland, 1987.

60. CAJ, 1990, at 13. Vote of May 1982 was 100 votes to 43 in favour of banning the use of plastic bullets in the EC.

61. For details see Fr Denis Faul and Fr Raymond Murray, *Plastic bullets — plastic government*, and *Rubber and plastic bullets kill and maim*, International Tribunal against rubber and plastic bullets, 1982.

62. CAJ, 1990, at 3.

63. *Adding Insult to Injury? Allegations of Harassment and the use of Lethal Force by the Security Forces in Northern Ireland*, CAJ, 1993, at 4.

64. *Ibid.*

65. *Troops Out*, "Plastic Bullets Campaign Triumph", July 1988.

66. *Irish News*, "'Yobs' started riot: residents", 1 October 1994.

67. *Irish News*, "Man hit by plastic bullet in hotel disturbance", 24 October 1994.

68. *Hansard*, Prevention of Terrorism (Temporary Provisions) Bill, 25 November 1974, col 882.

69. *The Prevention of Terrorism Act, A Liberty Briefing*, National Council for Civil Liberties, 1993, at 2.

70. *Ibid.*, at 1-3.

71. Sir Robert Mark, *In the office of constable, an autobiography*, Collins, 1978, at 174.

72. From *Statistics on the operation of prevention of terrorism legislation 1993*, Home Office Statistical Bulletin, 25 February 1994, Tables 1, 2 and 7.

73. The offences included in calculating this table are: murder, attempted murder, conspiracy, and offences under the Explosive Substances Act and the Firearms Act.

74. Hillyard, 1993, at 123-127.

75. *Ibid.*, at 240.

76. *Ibid.*, at 95-196.

77. See *Civil Liberty Agenda,* "When they come for you in the morning", summer 1993.

78. Clive Walker, *The prevention of terrorism in British Law, second edition,* Manchester University Press, 1992, at 138.

79. For example, the McNulty family and Kate Magee, leaflets issued by support groups.

80. Lord Shackleton, *Review into the operation of the Prevention of Terrorism (Temporary Provisions) Acts 1974 and 1975,* HMSO, Cmnd 7324, 1978, paras 132-133.

81. Walker, 1992, at 141-144.

82. *Times,* Law Report, 1 September 1992.

83. *Review of the operation of the Prevention of Terrorism (Temporary Provisions) Act 1984 by the Viscount Colville of Culross QC* (The Colville Report), HMSO, 1987, at 52.

84. *R v Richardson and others, Times,* Law Report, 20 October 1989.

85. *Brogan v United Kingdom,* (1988) Series A, No 145B, at para 62.

86. *Brannigan and MacBride v United Kingdom,* 26 May 1993, No 14552/89.

87. Schedule 8 Paragraph 6(8) Police and Criminal Evidence Act 1984.

88. Hillyard, 1993, at 95-181.

89. Walker, 1992, at 170.

90. For example, *Report to the United Kingdom government on the visit to Northern Ireland carried out by the European Committee for the Prevention of Torture and Inhuman or Degrading Treatment or Punishment, from 20 to 29 July 1993,* Council of Europe, CPT, 14 March 1994.

91. David Brown, *Detention under the Prevention of Terrorism (Temporary Provisions) Act 1989: access to legal advice and outside contact,* Home Office Research and Planning Unit, paper 75, 1993, at 8-23.

92. *Ibid.*, at 39.

93. s15(9) Prevention of Terrorism (Temporary Provisions) Act 1989.

94. Schedule 1 Prevention of Terrorism (Temporary Provisions) Act 1989.

95. s2 Prevention of Terrorism (Temporary Provisions) Act 1989.

96. s3 Prevention of Terrorism (Temporary Provisions) Act 1989.

97. Walker, 1992, at 59.

98. The Colville Report, 1987, at 46.

99. s8 Prevention of Terrorism (Temporary Provisions) Act 1989.

100. For example, *Hansard*, Prevention and suppression of terrorism, 9 March 1994, col 312.

101. For details see *Emergency laws and the Irish in Britain, the case of John Matthews*, Britain and Ireland Human Rights Centre, 1993.

102. Complaints to Liberty's legal department.

103. Paul Sieghart, *The International Law of Human Rights*, Clarendon Press 1983, at 464. UK reservation to Article 12 of the ICCPR: "The Government of the United Kingdom reserve the right to interpret the provisions of article 12(1) relating to the territory of a State a applying separately to each of the territories comprising the United Kingdom and its dependencies".

104. *Ibid.*

105. *Guardian*, "Exclusions challenged", 5 March 1993.

106. *R v Secretary of State for the Home Department, Ex parte Adams, Times*, Law Report, 10 August 1994.

107. *R v Secretary of State for the Home Department ex parte Gallagher*, 10 February 1994, Court of Appeal, and R v Secretary of State for the Home Department ex parte McQuillan, 9 September 1994.

108. *Hansard*, Written Answer, 29 November 1994, col 552.

109. *Report of the Commission to consider legal procedures to deal with terrorist activities in Northern Ireland* (The Diplock Report), HMSO, Cmnd 5185, 1972.

110. *A briefing paper on the Northern Ireland (Emergency Provisions) Bill*, Committee on the Administration of Justice, undated, at 7.

111. *Ibid.*

112. *Lawless v Ireland* Appl No 332/56, (1961) 1 EHRR 15.

113. *Ireland v United Kingdom*, (1978) 2 EHRR 25.

114. ss16-26 Northern Ireland (Emergency Provisions) Act 1991.

115. s18 Northern Ireland (Emergency Provisions) Act 1991.

116. s28 Northern Ireland (Emergency Provisions) Act 1991. There are seven organisations proscribed under the EPA: the Irish Republican Army, Cumann na mBan, Fianna na hEireann, the Red Hand Commando, Saor Eire, the Ulster Freedom Fighters, the Ulster Volunteer Force, the Irish National Liberation Army, the Irish People's Liberation Organisation and the Ulster Defence Association.

117. There were 16 prosecutions in 1991, 15 in 1992 and 24 in 1993. *Fourth Periodic Report by the United Kingdom of Great Britain and Northern Ireland to the Human Rights Committee under Article 40 of the International Covenant on Civil and Political Rights*, 1994, paras 399-400.

118. *Northern Ireland Office, Guide to the Emergency Powers*, Belfast HMSO, undated, at 50-54.

119. s10(1) and s12 Northern Ireland (Emergency Provisions) Act 1991.

120. For example see Steven Greer and Anthony White, *Abolishing the Diplock Courts*, The Cobden Trust, 1986.

121. s76 Police and Criminal Evidence Act 1984.

122. *R v McCormick* [1977] Northern Ireland Reports 105. Cited in Kevin Boyle, Tom Hadden and Paddy Hillyard, *Ten years on in Northern Ireland, the legal control of political violence*, The Cobden Trust, 1980, at 47.

123. For details see Peter Taylor, *Beating the terrorists? interrogations in Omagh, Gough and Castlereagh*, Penguin Books, 1980, and Dermot Walsh, *The use and abuse of emergency legislation in Northern Ireland*, Cobden Trust, 1983.

124. *Ireland v United Kingdom* (1978) 2 EHRR 25.

125. Amnesty International, *Report of a mission to Northern Ireland*, 1978.

126. *Report of the Committee of Inquiry into Police Interrogation Procedures in Northern Ireland* (the Bennett Report), HMSO Cmnd 7497, 1979.

127. Amnesty International, *United Kingdom, human rights concerns*, 1991, at 4.

128. *Summary Record of 92nd Meeting of UN Committee on Torture*, November 1991.

129. *Report to the government of the United Kingdom on the visit carried out by the European Committee for the Prevention of Torture and Inhuman or Degrading Treatment or Punishment*, Council of Europe, CPT/Inf(94) 17, 17 November 1994.

130. Anthony Jennings (Ed), *Justice under fire, the abuse of civil liberties in Northern Ireland*, Pluto Press, 1990, at 78.

131. For details see Tony Gifford QC, *The supergrasses, the use of accomplice evidence in Northern Ireland*, The Cobden Trust, 1984.

132. *Ibid.*

133. For details see Amnesty International, *United Kingdom, Northern Ireland: killings by security forces and "supergrass" trials*, 1988.

134. *Guardian*, "King ends right to silence", 21 October 1988.

135. *R v McCann* [1991] 92 Cr App 239

136. See for example *New Law Journal*, "The case of the Winchester Three", 9 February 1990.

137. *R v McCann* [1991] 92 Cr App 239.

138. *Hansard*, Northern Ireland, 8 November 1988, cols 182-223.

139. *Ibid.*, col 183.

140. *Hansard*, Northern Ireland, 8 November 1988, col 182. See also *Note by the Standing Advisory Committee on Human Rights on the Government's recent announcements affecting Northern Ireland dealing with terrorism and terrorist-related activities*, SACHR, 19 January 1989, at 3-5.

141. For details see James Wood and Adam Crawford, *The right of silence*, Civil Liberties Trust, 1989.

142. Articles 3 and 4 Criminal Evidence (Northern Ireland) Order 1988.

143. *Ibid.*

144. *Ibid.*

145. For details see *The Casement trials*, CAJ, 1992.

146. *R v Murray and others*, (CA) 7 July 1992.

147. *Murray v United Kingdom*, 27 June 1994, Appl No 18731/91.

148. *Ibid.*

149. For details see *The Casement trials*, CAJ, 1992.

150. For details see Ellen Weaver, *Right of silence debate: the Northern Ireland experience*, Justice, 1994.

151. *Commentary on the Northern Ireland Criminal Statistics*, Northern Ireland Office, 1993, at 15.

152. Weaver, 1994, at 4.

153. *Ibid.*, summary of conclusions.

154. *Ibid.*, at 36.

155. *Ibid.*, at 12.

156. *Hansard* (HL), Royal Assent, 3 November 1994, col 921. Not all the provisions come into force immediately. Abolition of the right of silence is due to come into effect in spring 1995, once a new caution has been formalised.

157. s76(1) Criminal Justice and Public Order Act 1994.

158. s76(4) Criminal Justice and Public Order Act 1994.

159. *Policing*, "Road block", summer 1994.

160. Complaints received by Liberty's legal department.

161. Letter from the City of London Police, 10 January 1994, forwarded to Liberty's legal office.

162. *Operation of Certain Police Powers Under PACE, England and Wales 1993*, Home Office Statistical Bulletin, Issue 15/94, Table 1. See also bulletins 14/91, 15/92 and 21/93.

163. *Ibid.*

164. s82(16) Criminal Justice and Public Order Act 1994.

165. s82(16)(1)(a) Criminal Justice and Public Order Act 1994.

166. For details see Laurence Lustgarten and Ian Leigh, *In from the cold, national security and parliamentary democracy*, Clarendon Press, 1994.

167. Stella Rimmington, *Security and democracy — is there a conflict?*, The Richard Dimbleby Lecture, 1994.

168. *Ibid.*

169. *Ibid.*

170. *Kurdistan Report*, "MI5, Special Branch and the criminalisation of the Kurds in Britain", January/February 1995.

171. Stella Rimmington, *James Smart Lecture*, 3 November 1994.

172. *Ibid.*

173. Rupert Allason, *The Branch, a history of the Metropolitan police special branch 1883-1983*, Secker & Warburg, 1983, at 1-16.

174. *R v McGonagle and Heffernan*, unreported.

175. *An Phoblacht/Republican News*, "Did MI5 let bombs go off to secure its role", 27 October 1994.

176. *Times*, Law Report, 17 August 1994.

177. *Ibid*.

178. *Guardian*, "Anonymous MI5 witness denies 'sight-seeing tour'", 8 December 1994.

179. s2 Security Service Act 1989.

180. ss2 and 4 Intelligence Services Act 1994.

181. *Guardian*, "MI5 hacks way in to publicise", 19 October 1994.

182. *Independent*, "Special Branch to target protesters", 3 November 1994.

183. Richard Norton Taylor, *In defence of the realm, the case for accountable security services*, Civil Liberties Trust, 1990, at 46.

184. *Ibid*., at 48.

185. *Guardian*, "Big brother's invisible men", 15 June 1985.

186. Norton Taylor, 1990, at 66.

187. BBC Radio, *File on Four*, 10 August 1982.

188. Norton Taylor, 1990, at 47-48.

189. *Hansard*, Written Answer, 7 March 1988, col 73.

190. *The Security Service*, HMSO July 1993, at 7-11.

191. *The Modern Law Review*, "The Intelligence Services Act 1994", November 1994.

192. *Ibid*.

193. s10 Intelligence Services Act 1994.

194. For details see Rowthorne and Wayne, *Northern Ireland: political economy of the conflict*, Polity, 1988.

195. For details see Bew, Gibbon and Patterson, *The State in Northern Ireland 1921-72: political forces and social classes*, Manchester University Press, 1979.

196. Wade and Bradley, *Constitutional and administrative law, eleventh edition* (by Bradley and Ewing), Longman, 1993, at 49.

197. For details see, for example, O'Leary, Lyne, Marshall and Rowthorn, *Northern Ireland, sharing authority*, Institute for Public Policy Research, 1993.

198. See Bridgid Hadfield (Ed), *The Northern Ireland Constitution*, Open University Press, 1992, at 6-11.

199. *Fortnight*, "Aloof in quangoland", January 1995.

200. Joint Declaration, 15 December 1993.

201. *Frameworks for the future*, HMSO Northern Ireland, 20 February 1995.

202. For example *The states we are in, civil rights in Ireland, north and south, the proceeds of a conference held in Trinity College, Dublin on 30 January 1993*, ICCL and CAJ, 1993.

203. Interviews with author, September 1994. See also *A bill of rights for Northern Ireland*, CAJ, 1993.

204. The Standing Advisory Commission on Human Rights was created by s20 of the Northern Ireland Constitution Act 1973 as a purely advisory body.